conomic Migrants

DAVE DALTON

Heinemann
LIBRARY

www.heinemann.co.uk/library
Visit our website to find out more information about Heinemann Library books.

To order:
 Phone 44 (0) 1865 888066
 Send a fax to 44 (0) 1865 314091
 Visit the Heinemann Bookshop at www.heinemann.co.uk/library to browse our catalogue and order online.

First published in Great Britain by Heinemann Library, Halley Court, Jordan Hill, Oxford OX2 8EJ, part of Harcourt Education.
Heinemann is a registered trademark of Harcourt Education Ltd.

© Harcourt Education Ltd 2006

First published in paperback in 2007
The moral right of the proprietor has been asserted.

Editorial: Jilly Attwood and Kathy Peltan
Design: Ron Kamen and Celia Jones
Illustrations: Jeff Edwards
Picture Research: Ruth Blair and Kay Altwegg
Production: Séverine Ribierre

Originated by Modern Age
Printed and bound in China by South China Printing Company

The paper used to print this book comes from sustainable resources.
10 digit ISBN 0 431 01382 9 (hardback)
13 digit ISBN 978 0 431 01382 4 (hardback)
10 09 08 07 06
10 9 8 7 6 5 4 3 2 1
10 digit ISBN 0 431 01386 1 (paperback)
13 digit ISBN 978 0 431 01386 2 (paperback)
11 10 09 08 07
10 9 8 7 6 5 4 3 2 1

British Library Cataloguing in Publication Data
Dalton, Dave
Economic Migrants
  (People on the Move)
  304.8'1
A full catalogue record for this book is available from the British Library.

Acknowledgements
The publishers would like to thank the following for permission to reproduce photographs:
Alamy p.**35**; Corbis pp.**21, 31**, p.**9**(Tiziana and Gianni Baldizzoni), p.**25**(Ed Kashi), p.**36**(Setboun Michel), p.**40**(David Turnley), p.**42**(Gideon Mendel); Getty Images pp.**5**(AFP), pp.**16, 17, 19, 23, 29, 30**(Hulton Archive), p.**28**(photodisc); Hulton Archive p.**33**; Mary Evans Picture Library p.**38**; Mary Evans/Town and Country Planning p.**23**; Oxfam(Jose-Luis Quintano) p.**27**; Panos Pictures pp.**6**(Betty Press), p.**45**(Penny Tweedie); Still Pictures(Markus Matzel) p.**13**;Topham/Image Works p.**43**; Trish Bartley p.**13**.

Cover photograph of a parent and child sitting on their bags at Shanghai railway station reproduced with permission of Imagine/China.

The publishers would like to thank Angus Willson, Director, Worldaware for his assistance in the preparation of this book.

Every effort has been made to contact copyright holders of any material reproduced in this book. Any omissions will be rectified in subsequent printings if notice is given to the publishers.

Contents

Words appearing in bold, **like this,** are explained in the glossary.

chapter one

Introduction

How would you feel?

Can you imagine leaving your home and family to move hundreds or thousands of miles away for a job? Perhaps you can. Perhaps someone from your family or a friend has done this.

What if one of your family moved for work and you did not know if you would ever see them again? Or can you picture your parents taking you and your family to a place you have never seen and know little about? Could you leave behind your friends and neighbours, your home, and most of your possessions, taking only what you could carry? It is a big step. It is a step from the life you know, to a new life that you hope will be better. It might sound exciting, but it could also be worrying, frightening, perhaps even dangerous.

Reasons and choices

Yet all through history, and right now as you read this, people have taken and are taking this big step. Sometimes people have no choice. They may be fleeing for their lives because of war. Perhaps they are escaping from persecution because of their religion, ethnic origin, or political views. Perhaps they are escaping from a flood, a drought, or an erupting volcano.

In this book we will look at **economic migration**. A country's **economy** is created by the work people do, the money they spend, and the goods and services they produce. Economic migration means that people move to a place where they think they will make a better living. Or they move because they can no longer make a living where they are. These are push and pull factors, which are explained more fully in the following chapters.

We will look at different reasons for **migration**, with examples and case studies of real migrations. Migration is usually a personal decision, and each migrant may have several reasons for moving. Starting from the same village, some people might travel to the nearest town, some to the other side of the world. And different kinds of migration can be happening at the same time, so a country could be gaining **immigrants** and losing **emigrants**.

A Chinese peasant makes her way along a street in Beijing in search of work. She is taking all her belongings with her.

What is migration?

Migration is the movement of people, especially in large numbers, to settle in a different place. Migration is as old as the human race. People have always moved around, ever since we first moved out from Africa and into the world's habitable places. When we talk about migrants, we do not mean tourists and explorers. Migrants move in large numbers, sometimes by the million. Often whole families move together, or the wage earners go first and their families join them later. And most migration is permanent. The migrants stay in their new home.

Consider this:
pack your bag

What would you take with you if you could take only one bag? Should you pack as much as you can carry, or travel light? Would you take only practical items, or include sentimental ones to remind you of home? What about food for the journey? Will you be able to buy what you need when you arrive? Who could you ask for advice? Parents have to take these decisions not just for themselves, but for their children ... and carry the children's things as well as their own.

Push and pull factors

To **migrate**, especially with all your family, and for ever, causes a huge upheaval. People do not do it on a whim. They have good reasons to make a move. Most **economic migrants** move because of a mixture of push factors and pull factors. There are problems with staying where they are, that push them away, and there are attractions about the place they go to, that pull them there. Sometimes the push factors are the stronger forces, and sometimes the pull factors are stronger.

Push factors

Few people would become economic migrants if they felt everything was fine where they were living. Sometimes things go wrong quite suddenly. For instance, if the biggest factory in town closes down and people are put out of work, with no hope of getting another job locally, that becomes a strong push factor.

Life has been hard for most people throughout history. It is still hard for most people today. There were about 1.2 billion people living on less than $1 a day in 1998. People endure poverty because they have to. They feel they have little or no choice. But there is a steady drift away of people who have finally had enough, or who see a chance of something better. We will see examples of both kinds of push factors in the following pages.

Pull factors

Few people would migrate unless they believed that life could be better in a new place. They may move because of definite news, such as the discovery of gold (see page 30). Quite often the information migrants have is vague, and they are travelling in hope. They go where they have heard there is land, there are jobs, and the **economy** is doing well. They follow friends, family, or neighbours who have migrated, done well, and written back to encourage them. Sometimes they are disappointed, and return home or even move further on, but most stay on and make the best of their new life. For most people, it is enough that the new place is better than the place they have left, even if it is not what they expected.

Consider this:
pushed or pulled?

Look around where you live and talk to your parents. Is it a prosperous place? Have things got better or worse in the last ten years? What could go wrong with the local economy? How bad would things have to get before people started thinking about moving? Where would they go? Or do you live in a part of the world which is pulling in economic migrants? Where have they come from? What have they come to do?

MIGRATION

Push factors	Pull factors
poverty	prosperity
unemployment	economic growth
low wages	jobs
population growth	high wages
land shortage	land

The comparison

If there is a big difference between the push factors and the pull factors, more people will migrate. They will be prepared to go further, and to endure more difficulties to get there. For desperate people, almost anything is better. For comfortable people, nothing much short of paradise will make them move. For some people, the decision is about the future. Even when things are bad, if they think they will get better, they may stay put. And if times are good but they think they will become bad, they may still decide to move.

People pushed from their homes by war sometimes stay on in their new country as economic migrants. Many Hutu families were displaced by the 1994 genocide in Rwanda and fled to Zaire.

chapter two

The push factors

Population growth

Since the beginning of human history the population has increased, and there has not always been enough land to support everyone. Also, when rich people own most of the land, poor people may not have enough land to support themselves. Some people have moved to find unoccupied land, or have squeezed into wherever there was room to make a living.

Population and poverty

In a farming country, population growth can leave people without land. Or they have such a small plot of land that they cannot grow enough food to eat or sell. In cities, there may be more people wanting to work than there are jobs to do. This means some are unemployed, and others work for low wages. The result is the same – poverty. Poverty is the push factor that makes people become **economic migrants.**

Sometimes many people move at about the same time. For example, if there is an **economic depression** and workers lose their jobs, many will move. More often there is a steady trickle of people who have finally decided not to put up with hard times any longer. Landless families may be forced out of the countryside into cities within their own country. Or they may leave their country and travel further, to find land or work in another country. European settlers **emigrated** in the 17th, 18th, and 19th centuries to North America. In the 19th and 20th centuries they also went to Australia, New Zealand, Argentina, and parts of Africa. Population growth in China caused Chinese **migration** to the USA and to more prosperous places in Asia, such as Malaya and Singapore. Japanese people migrated to the USA and Brazil.

Rising population and emigration
Britain in the 19th century

Years	Population growth	Number of emigrants per year
1801–1851	From 10 million to 20 million	1820s: about 30,000 1830: 60,000 1832: 100,000 1842: 130,000 1847–1849: 750,000
1851–1871	5 million	3,700,000

It may be better to be a casual labourer in a city than a landless labourer in the country. Rickshaw riders in Dhaka, the capital of Bangladesh, make their living by driving people around the city. Most of them do not own the rickshaws, but rent them by the day. Every day they earn enough to pay the rent, and hope there is enough left over to buy food.

Pushed into cities

Migration from the countryside to the city is one of the biggest types of migration happening today. In poor countries, population growth pushes people off the land and into cities. Population growth means that more people have little or no land. This is even more likely if some people have more land than others to begin with. Landless people in a poor country have to survive on whatever work their better-off neighbours will give them. This work is often very poorly paid, and only available at the busy times of the farming year. The poverty of landless people is a strong push factor. Things may not be much better in the city, but there are more opportunities, creating a pull factor. So poor, landless people from the country migrate to the cities.

Consider this:
family inequality

Picture yourself as the oldest child in a family which the father can barely support. Along comes one more child. What could you do to help? Now picture yourself as the youngest child in a farming family. When your father dies, the land is shared between your older brothers and there is none for you. What would you do?

Transmigration in Indonesia

Indonesia is a country made up of many islands. The government has been encouraging people to **migrate** from the most crowded islands to places where there is more room. They call this process **transmigration.**

Indonesia's population

Indonesia has the world's fourth largest population. In 2004, there were 238,450,000 people. It is also a poor country: the average income is $690 (£375) a year. Most people live on only a few of the islands. The islands of Java, Madura, and Bali make up only 7 per cent of Indonesia's land area, but in 1990 they had 69 per cent of the population.

Java

Java has rich, volcanic soils and a tropical climate. People can grow good crops of rice for their families. They also grow crops for sale. For example, coffee grows well higher up the mountain slopes. The island supports a big population, but this has been growing fast and now farming just cannot support any more people.

Indonesia is in green. As Java, Madura, and Bali are densely populated, the government has encouraged transmigration to the less populated islands.

Population density in Indonesia in 1990	
Island	Number of people per sq km (per sq mile)
Java	814 (1309)
Sumatra	77 (124)
Irian Jaya	4 (6)

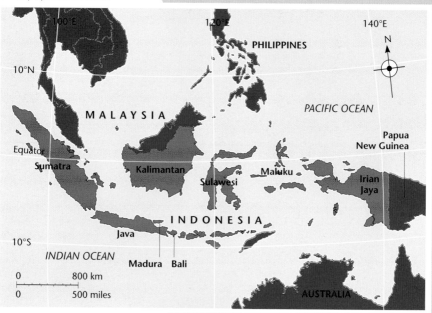

Transmigration

For many years the government
has encouraged people to
migrate from crowded Java to
other islands, especially Sumatra.
In the 21 years between 1949
and 1970, 1 million people
migrated away from Java. In the
five years between 1979 and 1984,
another 1.5 million migrated. These
figures include both 'unofficial' migration,
and people who moved under the
government's Transmigration Programme.
Between 1969 and 1989, this official programme
relocated about 730,000 families from Java, Bali, and Madura to less
populated islands. Nearly half of these migrants went to Sumatra. Smaller
numbers went to other 'importing' islands such as Kalimantan, Sulawesi,
Maluku, and Irian Jaya.

The government has encouraged migration for two reasons. First, to relieve
population pressure in the islands the migrants leave. Second, to develop
agriculture, forestry, and mining in the islands they move to.

Problems

Transmigration has not been a complete success. The population of Java is
still increasing. People are having more children than the number of migrants
leaving the island. In the 1980s, when the government was encouraging
migration, the population of Java increased by 18 per cent. Also, the settlers
on the other islands have struggled with their new surroundings. They have
had difficulties growing unfamiliar crops. They have also had to deal with
poor roads, water supply, schools, and health care. Up to 20 per cent of the
migrants have returned home. The people of the 'importing' islands often
oppose transmigration because they feel the migrants are taking their land.
Environmental organizations are concerned about the damage caused to the
environment of these islands by cutting down forests to create new farms.

Other options

The government has two other options to help support the growing
population. One is to redistribute land from those who have plenty, to those
who have little or none. This has not happened in Indonesia, for political
reasons. The other option is to encourage foreign firms to set up in Indonesia
to provide jobs in factories. There has been some success with this, although
wages are low and working conditions are often bad. People continue to
drift from the countryside to the cities in Indonesia, as in many other
developing countries.

The slave trade

Slavery has happened throughout history. Wherever slavery has existed, slaves have been traded from one place to another. For the slaves, their trade has been a forced **migration**. It was an **economic migration** because money was the reason for their movement. For the slaves it meant the loss of their liberty, leaving their families, and often brutal working conditions at their final destination. But the numbers involved were small, until European journeys to the **New World** and the exploration of Africa began.

The Atlantic triangle

From the 16th and 17th centuries European countries such as Spain, France, Portugal, and Britain set up **colonies** in the New World. The settlers started huge **plantations**, growing crops to sell back in Europe, such as sugar, coffee, cotton, and tobacco. They wanted slaves to do the hard work on these plantations. At about the same time, European explorers and traders were working their way down the west coast of Africa and setting up trading posts. They soon realized that one of the most profitable trades was to buy slaves to take to the New World. They bought them from African slave traders. The slaves had been captured in wars between African tribes, or in raids on villages by slave traders.

The arrows on this map illustrate the Atlantic triangle. Goods were bought in Europe and traded for slaves in Africa. Slaves were then taken to the New World and sold.

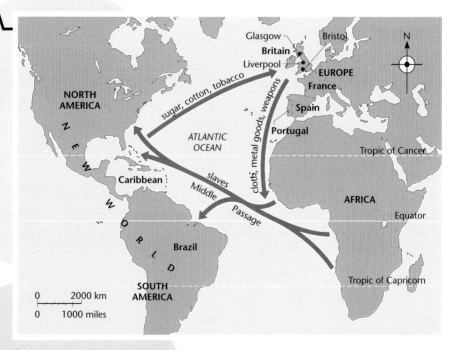

A triangular trade grew up. From Europe, ships took cloth, metal goods, and weapons to Africa, which were traded for slaves. The second side of the triangle, known as the Middle Passage, took the slaves across the Atlantic Ocean from Africa to the New World. The slaves were chained below decks in horribly overcrowded conditions. The trading ships completed the triangle by returning to Europe with cargoes of sugar, cotton, and tobacco, which had been grown by the slaves. One estimate is that 9 million slaves crossed the Atlantic between 1648 and 1815. Up to 20 per cent of the slaves died during the crossing, from ill-treatment or disease. By the end of the trade, there were 1.5 million slaves in the southern United States, 1 million in the Caribbean, and 2 million in Brazil. Black people now form the majority of the population in the Caribbean, and a large minority in many other countries of North and South America.

Profit – and abolition

The slave trade was dominated in the 17th century by the Dutch, and in the 18th century by the British. The British cities Glasgow, Liverpool, and Bristol became prosperous largely because of the Atlantic slave trade. By the end of the 18th century, there were about 10,000 slaves in England. They were mostly employed as domestic servants. But public opinion turned against the cruelties of slavery and the slave trade. In 1772 it was made illegal to own slaves in Britain. In 1807 Britain made the trade in slaves illegal. In 1808 the United States banned the importation of slaves. Slavery and slave trading remained legal in the southern states of the USA until 1865. As settlers moved west, they took slaves with them.

Slavery still exists and campaigns against it continue.

STOP!

SLAVERY IN SUDAN

Consider this:
modern slavery

You may think that slavery and slave trading are things of the past. But there is still an illegal trade taking people from poor countries to richer ones. They are made to work as servants or in the sex industry. Their conditions can only be described as slavery. In 2004, it was reported that 25,000 people were working as slave labourers in Brazil.

The Great Migration

Many of the descendants of the African slaves made a second **migration** within the USA. This Great Migration, as it is sometimes called, was to escape poverty and **discrimination** in the southern states.

Discrimination and poverty

When slavery was abolished in the USA in 1865, the African-American people of the southern states got their freedom, but not much else. The white people passed laws to prevent African Americans from voting. The freed slaves were denied justice, **civil rights**, and dignity. They had to use separate schools, eating places, and toilets, and to sit at the back on buses. In addition to this **segregation** and discrimination, they also suffered poverty.

In **rural** areas, African Americans had poorly paid farm jobs. If they farmed for themselves, they used land that belonged to someone else and paid rent in the form of a share of the crop. The very poorest relied on the landowner not just for land, but for seed, tools, and the mule to pull the plough. Many got into debts with the landowner, which they could never repay.

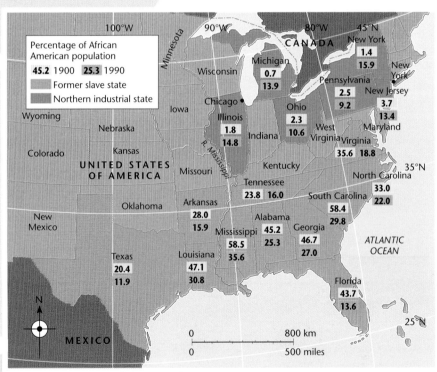

This map shows population changes between 1900 and 1990 in former slave states and in the northern industrial states.

Push and pull factors

This double burden of poverty and discrimination in the rural south created a powerful push factor. There was also a strong pull factor from the **industrial** cities of the north, where African Americans could find better-paid jobs and civil rights. Even here they did not escape from racial prejudice. But they could vote, and their children could go to school, and they had a better chance of sharing work-places, schools, public places, and buses with white people as equals.

Moving north

When African Americans migrated from south to north, they did not cross any borders, so there are no official records of how many people moved. One estimate is that over 600,000 African Americans moved north during the 1920s alone. But we can see, from the government census figures, the scale of this migration. Between 1910 and 1920, the African-American population of Mississippi fell from 1,009,000 to 935,000. The number in Michigan rose from 17,000 to 60,000. Over the next ten years that number rose to 169,000.

The proportion of African-American people in the total population of the USA hardly changed at all. It was 11.6 per cent in 1900 and 12.1 per cent in 1990. But the number of African Americans living in the former slave states fell, and the African-American percentage of the population of northern industrial states rose.

Consider this:
the turning of the tide

Things have now changed in the south, and the pattern of push and pull factors is different. African Americans are moving back to cities in the southern states, from the north and west.

State	Change in African-American population, 1995-2000
New York	- 165,366
California	- 63,180
Illinois	- 55,238
Georgia	+ 129,749
North Carolina	+ 53,371
Florida	+ 51,286

Unemployment and poverty

Unemployment causes poverty and creates a powerful push factor. People **migrate** to look for jobs. The clearest examples of this sort of migration come from the Great Depression of the 1930s. It started in the USA and the Case Study overleaf looks at its effects there. Here we see how the Depression hit the people of Britain.

Causes of unemployment

Economies go through ups and downs. There are good times, sometimes called booms, when there is plenty of work. In hard times, often called **economic depressions**, there are high levels of unemployment. On top of this, particular industries have ups and downs. When cars began to replace horse-drawn vehicles, there was a boom for the car industry. But industries making wagons and harnesses went into decline. Another cause of job losses can be when one country's industry loses its market to cheaper products from another country. Add all these together, and even in boom times there will be places where most workers are employed in an industry in decline. Even in times of general depression, some places will be worse off than others.

Chain of suffering

When people lose their jobs, they live on their savings, if they have any. When the savings run out, they sell their possessions. They also cut their spending on everything, but bare necessities. Sooner or later they start to think about leaving home to look for work in a more prosperous part of the country. The problem is worse when virtually a whole town or city relies on one industry. If that closes down, there is little chance of finding another job. As unemployed people cut their spending, small local businesses suffer. Soon the people working in these businesses lose their jobs too.

Britain in the Depression of the 1930s

Unemployment reached its worst in the UK in 1932. Nearly 23 per cent of the working-age population was unemployed. That meant 3.75 million people. Unemployment levels in some industries were even worse:
- shipbuilding   59.5 per cent
- iron and steel   48.5 per cent
- coal   41.2 per cent
- cotton   31.1 per cent.

Because those industries were concentrated in certain places, the pattern of unemployment also varied from one region to another:
- London and south-east England   13.7 per cent
- Northern England   27.1 per cent
- Wales   36.5 per cent
- Scotland   27.7 per cent
- Northern Ireland   27.2 per cent.

The contrast was even sharper between particular towns. In 1934 Jarrow, a shipbuilding town in northern England, had 67.8 per cent unemployment. Oxford, in southern England, with a booming car industry, had 5.1 per cent.

Migration

Over 1 million people of working age migrated to south-east England from the 'depressed areas' between 1921 and 1939. Wales alone lost 450,000 people. London and its suburbs increased in population from 7.5 million in 1921 to 8.5 million by 1939, and cities such as Birmingham and Coventry, with prosperous car industries, also gained migrants looking for work.

Consider this: what should the government do?

The British Government could not do much about the Depression. But they encouraged people to move for work. When so many people moved, they left behind empty houses, and local schools and hospitals were under-used. In the booming areas there was a rush to build more houses, schools, hospitals, and roads. The government also encouraged new industries to set up in the areas of high unemployment.

These unemployed workers are taking a break during a protest march from Scotland to London in May 1930. They hoped to raise people's awareness of the economic depression in Scotland.

Unemployment in the USA in the 1930s

In October 1929, **share** prices on the American **Stock Market** collapsed. Panic spread through the **economy** and the price of goods fell. A vicious circle set in. Workers lost their jobs. Firms would not take on workers because they saw no market for their goods. There was no market for goods because unemployed people could not afford to buy them. The Great Depression had begun.

Unemployment increases

By December 1932, the level of unemployment had reached 25 per cent. Unemployed people had no income at all. Once they had spent their savings and sold their possessions, they had nothing and had to rely on charity. Some people who had lost their homes lived in cardboard shacks.

Date	Number of unemployed people in the USA
1929	1.5 million
March 1930	3.25 million
December 1930	5 million
December 1931	9 million
December 1932	13 million

Poor farmers

The Great Depression also devastated farmers. They were hit by low prices for crops. Farm incomes fell by 60 per cent between 1929 and 1932. Many farmers were unable to pay their debts and lost their farms to the bank.

A map of population change and unemployment in the USA, 1930–1940.

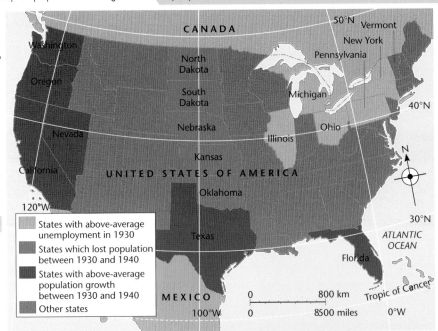

States with above-average unemployment in 1930

States which lost population between 1930 and 1940

States with above-average population growth between 1930 and 1940

Other states

The completion of San Francisco's Golden Gate Bridge in 1937 symbolized the growth and optimism of California in the 1930s.

Recovery and growth areas

From about 1933, things slowly began to get better. The government did what it could to help. Confidence returned, businesses hired workers, so workers had money to spend. Even so, by 1937 industry was still only working at 75 per cent of its 1929 level. The recovery was strongest in the new industries, such as aircraft and electrical goods. These often started up in areas away from the traditional centres of industry. The economic growth areas included California, Washington state, south Texas, and Detroit, where the car industry was reviving.

Migration

Between 1930 and 1940, the population of the USA grew by 8.9 million. There was hardly any immigration, so this growth was by natural increase, at just over 7 per cent over ten years. But six states lost population. They were Kansas, Nebraska, North Dakota, Oklahoma, South Dakota, and Vermont. People **migrated** out, because of the push factors of unemployment and rural poverty.

States with unemployment rates below the national average also had population growth above the national average, because of people migrating in. These states included Florida, Nevada, Oregon, Texas, and Washington. The biggest growth was in California, which gained 1.23 million people. Most of these were migrants, attracted by California's prosperity.

Consider this: push, pull, and stay

Faced with the poverty caused by the Great Depression, many people chose to stay put and wait for better times. Others decided to migrate, pushed by unemployment and poverty. Economic growth areas with low unemployment had strong pull factors, and California was the strongest of all.

chapter three

The pull factors

The pull of city life

There was a time when nearly everyone lived in the country. For country people, life changed little from year to year. Every season had its work, such as sowing, weeding, and harvesting the crops. Every day had its routine of feeding the animals and milking the cows. It was hard work, with long hours, outside in all weathers.

Sounds boring? Maybe you would have been one of the restless people who left a good life in the country to seek out a better one in the city. Towns and cities have always offered a wider range of ways to make a living than the countryside.

Crafts

Craft workers of all kinds live in cities, where there are plenty of people to buy their products. They include weavers, tailors, potters, jewellers, carpenters, painters, writers, actors, and musicians, software writers, and website designers. Anyone with a skill will be drawn to a city where they can make a living doing what they are good at. Businesses often congregate together, and create work for other businesses: furniture-makers need hinges, handles, paint, and polish, and tailors need fabric, buttons, needles, and thread.

Professions

Other jobs appear around the centres of power, education, and religion in cities. They include soldiers, priests, politicians, police, lawyers, writers, teachers, doctors, scientists, and journalists. People in these lines of business rely on each other: politics and court cases give the media something to report on and discuss, and authors write books, to keep publishers, printers, and bookshops busy.

Trade

Cities are centres of trade. Hotels, restaurants, shops, banks, and docks provide a chance to travel, meet people, take risks, and make money. Buses, trains, ferries, taxis, and planes get people around, and running them creates more jobs. Marketing and advertising agencies, postal workers, and telephone engineers help to keep businesses running.

In recent years traffic congestion, crime, and expensive house prices have made big cities in rich countries less attractive places to live. The streets may be 'paved with gold', but you cannot see them for parked cars.

Rich and poor

If things go well, you may make a fortune and create a business employing lots of people. Spending your fortune provides jobs for the people working in your household, and for those making your luxury goods. If you do not make a fortune, you will probably still be able to make a living. Someone has to empty the bins, wash the dishes, and sweep the streets. Cities even provide better opportunities for beggars, gamblers, buskers, confidence tricksters, and criminals.

Consider this: back to the country?

In rich countries, technology such as telephones and computers make it possible to do some big-city jobs while living in the country. Some people are leaving expensive and crowded cities to live in the country. What effects will this have on cities and towns? How will it help the transport services? What will happen to the shops and services that rely on passing trade?

Industrialization

Until about 200 years ago, towns grew slowly. People gradually moved into them either drawn by the town's promise, or pushed out of the countryside by poverty. Then, when countries began the process of industrialization, the rate of growth speeded up. People **migrated** in huge numbers. Towns became cities, and cities became huge.

Industrial revolution

In an **industrial** revolution, a country's **economy** changes very quickly. Instead of most people working in **agriculture** and living in the country, most people work in industry and live in towns and cities. Different countries have gone through this change at different times. Britain was first, in the 18th century. The process is still happening in some **developing countries** today. In industrialized countries people work in factories, using machines to produce goods. Quicker production means cheaper goods, and cheaper goods mean bigger markets. The factory owners make good profits, some of which they invest in building more factories.

Migration

The booming factories need lots of new workers. People may work long hours for low wages, perhaps in dangerous conditions. Even so, they migrate to the cities for these jobs. The push factors are population growth and poverty in the countryside. The pull factor is the hope of a steady job in the city.

The growth of cities in Britain

In 1815 most English families worked on the land or lived in small towns. The capital city, London, however, already had more than 1 million people. By 1830, Birmingham and Sheffield had doubled in size, and Liverpool, Leeds, Manchester, and Glasgow had more than doubled. By a combination of population growth and continued migration from the countryside, the cities continued to grow.

City	Population in 1841	Population in 1881
London	2 million	5 million
Sheffield	111,000	285,000
Nottingham	52,000	187,000
Salford	53,000	176,000

Between 1851 and 1861 seven **rural** English counties lost population, and between 1871 and 1891 so did another five. People left agricultural work in country areas to find work in factories.

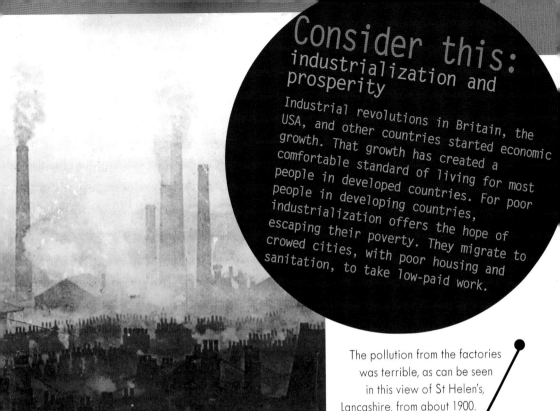

Consider this: industrialization and prosperity

Industrial revolutions in Britain, the USA, and other countries started economic growth. That growth has created a comfortable standard of living for most people in developed countries. For poor people in developing countries, industrialization offers the hope of escaping their poverty. They migrate to crowed cities, with poor housing and sanitation, to take low-paid work.

The pollution from the factories was terrible, as can be seen in this view of St Helen's, Lancashire, from about 1900.

The Industrial Revolution in the USA

The Industrial Revolution spread to other European countries and to the USA. In 1860, four out of five Americans lived in the country. Between 1860 and 1900 the USA industrialized fast. New industrial cities attracted people from the countryside, and also from Europe. Even so, 25 per cent of the USA's population still lived on farms in 1930. We will see more about migration to the USA, and within it, on pages 24–25 and 28–31.

These workers of 1890 are from the blast furnace at Ensley, near Birmingham, Alabama in the USA. The furnace converted raw iron into **pig iron**.

Industry and migration in the USA

As technology changes, new industries set up in new places, and people move to follow the jobs. In the USA, both **immigrants** and **internal migrants** moved in response to these pull factors.

Changing industry

New inventions, discoveries, and technologies create new industries. Iron was followed by steel, then steel by aluminium and plastic. Railways replaced canals, then came cars, lorries, and planes. Early factories used water power for their machines, so they were sited next to rivers. When coal-fired machines powered industry, there were many jobs in coal mines, and some industries moved to be near the coal. Now industry uses oil, natural gas, and electricity. Pipelines and cables deliver power all over the country, so industries are not tied to coalfields.

Westward migration

Europeans first settled on the east coast of North America early in the 17th century. From then until the country's **industrial** revolution, people tended to move west. Sometimes they were internal migrants, sometimes immigrants, looking for land. Land has always had a big attraction for people in the USA. Even if they already had a farm in the east of the country, a family would be tempted to move west for better land, more land, or free land. The 'frontier' between settled and empty land moved steadily westward during the 19th century.

Industry in the north-east

In the last third of the 19th century, industry began to grow in the east and the midwest. Big cities, such as Chicago and Cleveland, grew on the Great Lakes. Others, such as New York and Philadelphia, grew around ports, or on coalfields, such as Pittsburgh. Many immigrants from Europe found jobs in the growing cities. For a few decades, the big cities in the north-east slowed down the westward-moving trend of the population. In 1900, nine of the ten most highly populated states were in the north-east. The exception was Texas.

Industry in the west

In the early 20th century, California was a prosperous **agricultural** state with a big port city, San Francisco. Los Angeles, in the south of the state, was starting to grow. In 1911 a cinema studio opened in Hollywood. Oil had been discovered on the coast near Los Angeles, and by the 1920s Los Angeles was the world's largest oil port. Aircraft manufacturing arrived in the 1930s. California grew faster than any other part of the country in the 1930s. It continued to prosper and draw in migrants throughout the 20th century. By 2000 it was the most highly populated state, with Texas second. Los Angeles is one of the world's largest cities, and its **economy** is bigger than that of India.

Aerial view of Oracle headquarters in Silicon Valley, 1999.
The company has been a major provider of business software since 1977.

Silicon Valley

The computer and software industries need intelligent, creative people. They are likely to be university educated, and so computer industries have often clustered around universities. One of these clusters is Silicon Valley. This is the name given to the booming and fast-growing towns around Stanford University, in Palo Alto, 56 kilometres (35 miles) south of San Francisco. Hewlett-Packard, Oracle, Adobe, Intel, Apple, Sun, Google, NASA, and Lockheed Martin are all located here, on the shores of the Pacific Ocean.

Consider this:
still moving

Between 2000 and 2003 the population of the United States increased by 3.3 per cent. North Dakota and the District of Columbia lost population. Of the top ten fastest-growing states, six were in the west, and four in the south. People are still moving around the country, but perhaps the pull of the west is now less strong.

The lure of land

In Bolivia, South America, people are on the move to find good land and a better living. The Andes mountains run through the west of Bolivia. For thousands of years people have lived on the dry, rocky plateau called the *altiplano*, which means 'high plain'. As the population has grown, there is not enough land for everyone to support themselves. The tin-mining industry, which used to provide jobs in the towns, has collapsed. Most people are very poor.

Eastward migration

People are on the move from the *altiplano* to the lowlands in the east of the country. They are pulled by the lure of free land. The lowlands have a hot, wet climate. They are part of the Amazon rainforest. The area is thinly inhabited by **indigenous** people who live by hunting and gathering wild food.

The government has cut a long, straight road through the forest. A bus service runs from the nearest city, Santa Cruz. The bus brings in everything people need, such as clothes, tools, and medicine. By the mid-1990s tens of thousands of **migrants** had moved there. They cleared the trees to grow rice and maize, and to keep chickens and pigs.

Here to stay

It is hard work to clear the forest. People are not used to the hot, humid climate, or to the mosquitoes. But they stay because they can have all the land they want. At first, they built their homes of timber and thatch, using forest materials, and got water from wells. But now some buildings are of brick and tile, and some homes have piped water. A line of market stalls along the main road is the beginning of a town. The migrants are here to stay.

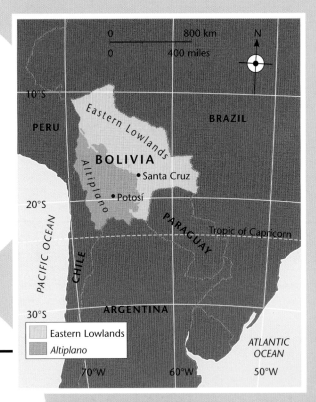

This map of Bolivia, shows the *altiplano* and the eastern lowland areas.

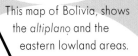

Gerardo's story

Gerardo Pirca Gandia, his wife and their eight children moved to the village of Nueva Jordania eight years ago. They came from Potosí, a tin-mining town in the Andes. They were penniless when they arrived, but by growing rice on ten hectares of land they have prospered. Gerardo now has fifteen sheep, fourteen cows, and a horse. "Life is better here than in Potosí. The mosquitoes get me down, and we have floods, but I'm doing very well here, I don't miss Potosí."

Sometimes it rains so much in the tropical lowlands of eastern Bolivia that the rivers flood. This family of migrants is walking along what used to be the road.

Consider this:
environmental consequences

The migration of people to the lowlands, and the clearance of forest to create space for farming, will seriously affect the environment. Consider the issues connected to this case study. What will be lost by cutting down large areas of the rainforest? How will this affect the world's climate? What will happen to the indigenous people? How can the number of migrants entering this area be controlled? Discover more about the environmental issues in People on the Move: Environmental Migration.

The land of opportunity

Forty million Europeans migrated to the USA, or to the **colonies** that were to become the USA, between 1607 and 1914. Thirty-five million of them made the journey between 1815 and 1914, to start a new life in the **New World**. This was the largest peaceful **migration** in recorded history.

Push factors

All the migrants were pushed by poverty, but for some there was the extra push of oppression and **persecution** in their home country. In the first half of the 19th century, the main sources of migrants were Germany, Britain, and Ireland. A million people left Ireland during and after the Potato Famine of 1845–1849. Later in the 19th century the biggest numbers of **emigrants** came from Poland and Italy.

Pull factors

The pull factors of land, economic opportunity, and freedom, drew millions of people. The economic attraction increased after industrialization. There were plenty of jobs in the new factories. For many migrants the pull of the USA was not just economic. It was also a land of freedom, a democracy with a constitution guaranteeing their **civil rights**.

Waves of migrants

The result of these pushes and pulls was three waves of **immigration** to the USA. The first ran from the 1830s to a high in 1854, when 427,833 people crossed the Atlantic. The second wave started in the 1870s and peaked at 788,992 people in 1882. The third wave brought an average of 1 million immigrants a year between 1905 and 1914.

Nearly 2 million Italians moved to the USA between 1898 and 1907. Between 1880 and 1920 a third of the Jews of Eastern Europe emigrated, 90 per cent of them moving to the USA. Over 1,500,000 Jews arrived between 1900 and 1914. They were fleeing poverty and religious persecution.

The statue of Liberty at the entrance to the harbour of New York greeted millions of immigrants to the USA. A plaque on the statue includes the words "Give me your tired, your poor, your huddled masses yearning to breathe free ..."

Migrants were usually young adults, so the welcoming country gained a person of working age. That helped the economy to grow, which attracted more adults. Emigrants also affected the countries they left, by reducing population pressure and the problem of poverty. What would the world be like if these great migrations had not happened?

Many immigrants started their new lives in crowded city slums.

An Irishman writing home from the USA, 1849.

"I am exceedingly well pleased at coming to this land of plenty. On arrival I purchased 120 acres of land at $5 an acre ... I would advise all my friends to quit Ireland – the country most dear to me; as long as they remain in it they will be in bondage and misery."

Destinations

Immigrants with little or no English naturally gathered together. Earlier migrants who had prospered could afford to help their friends and family join them. In Chicago in 1890, over 40 per cent of the city's population was foreign-born. In 1915 Chicago had the third largest urban Polish community in the world. Russian Jews settled particularly in New York, Chicago, and Philadelphia. New York's Lower East Side had 540,000 Jewish immigrants by the 1920s. Most big cities had Jewish, Irish, Polish, or Italian neighbourhoods. Immigrants from Norway and Sweden often started farms in Wisconsin and Minnesota, where land was opening up for settlement.

Gold rushes

When gold is discovered, the rush of people to make money out of it is an exciting, dramatic, but often short-lived form of **economic migration**. In a way, gold is not the point of gold rushes. When thousands of people start scouring the country for gold, not all of them will find it. Very few will make a fortune. But there will be money to be made, selling the prospectors what they need, building their lodgings and growing their food. When the excitement has passed, some unsuccessful prospectors may go home disappointed, but many more will stay on and find a living. So a gold rush brings in a mass of people, and people create work for each other. This is good for the local **economy**.

This 1846 photo shows Grunille's claim, a gold mine in California.

California

James Wilson Marshall, a carpenter, found gold in the waters of the American River in California in January 1848. As news of Marshall's discovery began to spread, gold fever swept the nation, and the world. Thousands of people rushed to California from around the world. Those who came from the eastern USA travelled by various sea routes or overland through country that had barely been explored, let alone settled. These were the routes that would later be used by settlers. Gold seekers flooded into San Francisco and other boom towns.

The 1848 Gold Rush was the start of California's economic and population growth. Eighty thousand migrants joined the 12,000 people already living there. By 1860 the population was nearly 380,000. By 1853 there were 25,000 Chinese people living in San Francisco, in the first "Chinatown" in the USA.

Other rushes in the USA

In the second half of the 19th century there were many more rushes, although not always for gold. Some died out quickly, other areas are still producing today. Some of these rushes were:

- 1859   silver in Colorado
- 1876   gold in the Black Hills of South Dakota
- 1878   gold and silver in Mammoth City, California
- 1896   gold in the Yukon territory of Canada, bringing 30,000 people to nearby Alaska.

Consider this:
gold – dream or nightmare?

Gold rushes attracted adventurous, desperate, even ruthless people, and there was crime and violence in the chaos of the gold-rush towns. Perhaps the safest way to make money was to sell food to the hungry miners. In the California gold rush, apples were selling for $5 each.

Rushes in other countries

Diamonds were discovered at Kimberley, South Africa, in 1867. By 1874 the town had 50,000 people. Gold was discovered at Dunedin in New Zealand in 1861, and at Witwatersrand in South Africa in 1886.

Ten thousand Australians went to California in 1849, and some returned, disappointed, to look for gold in their own country. They found rich deposits of gold in 1851 in the state of New South Wales. But they were soon outshone by Victoria state, where there were the richest goldfields the world had ever seen. In the next ten years, Victoria's population grew from 80,000 to 500,000. Melbourne, the capital of Victoria, grew from 23,000 people in 1850 to 126,000 in 1861. New South Wales rose from 190,000 to 350,000. Most of these new people came from Britain, but there were also 40,000 Chinese.

This is Sydney Cove, Australia, in 1803. This small settlement would be transformed by the gold rush later in the century.

The mother country

Many countries in western Europe became very prosperous in the 1950s and 1960s. Their prosperity created a pull factor for people in the **colonies** and ex-colonies of European countries. Even when colonies had become independent, their people had special rights of citizenship in the country that had colonized them. Britain was described as the 'mother country' to countries such as India, Pakistan, Bangladesh, and the West Indies.

The pull factors

In the booming **economies** of the 1950s there were plenty of jobs, especially if you were prepared to work unsocial hours, or for low wages. Many West Indians worked in Britain's National Health Service and public transport system. The other pull factor was the opportunity to get a better education for your children, in a country which you had always been encouraged to admire.

Immigration to Britain

The first 492 men arrived in Britain from Jamaica in 1948, on a ship called the *Empire Windrush*. By the mid-1950s, **immigrants** from the West Indies, India, and Pakistan were arriving in tens of thousands a year. The British government encouraged this **immigration**, because unemployment levels were low and it was difficult to fill the least popular jobs.

The immigrants were different from most people in Britain. The West Indians were descendants of African slaves taken to the Caribbean in the 17th and 18th centuries. They spoke English with distinctive accents. Migrants from India, Pakistan, and Bangladesh were ethnically Asian. Many spoke little or no English, and they were Hindus or Muslims. Like most immigrants, they kept together, living in the poorer parts of cities where housing was cheap. West Indians congregated in parts of London and in the cities of the West

In the 1950s and 1960s, large numbers of migrants went to Britain from the West Indies and areas highlighted in red on this map.

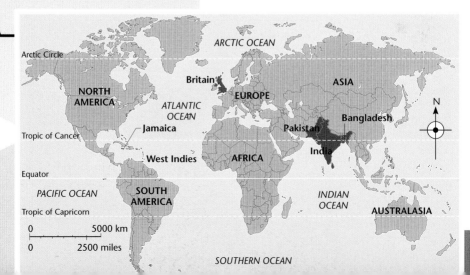

Midlands, such as Birmingham. Immigrants from India, Pakistan, and Bangladesh went to different neighbourhoods in London, and to cities such as Leicester and Bradford.

As a result of this **economic migration**, Britain now has a mixed population, with large racial and religious minorities. Many of them were born in Britain. By a combination of immigration and natural population growth among the immigrant communities, Britain now has 4.6 million people of non-white background, making up 7.9 per cent of the population. Nearly half of them live in London, where they make up 29 per cent of the city's population. Over the country as a whole, Indians are the largest group, followed by Pakistanis, people of mixed race, black Caribbeans, black Africans, and Bangladeshis. Another measure of the impact of these immigrants is that by 2001 Britain had 1.59 million Muslims, making up 2.7 per cent of the population.

The *Empire Windrush* was the first of many ships that brought migrants from the West Indies to Britain.

Clinton Edwards was among the first Jamaican emigrants to Britain, on the *Empire Windrush* in 1948.

"I first came to England during the war, in the RAF. When I went back home there was no work so I decided to come back. There was a boat coming back, by the name of Windrush and it was only £28, so I paid my fare and came back. My life in England has been very good, I enjoy my work, and my work mates, and they treat me nice. I have been back home several times on holiday. I still call Jamaica home, although I lost my parents, you know. The home is still there, my relatives live there, and I have to keep up with the repairs, but I prefer to live here. I am married, my family is here, my children, my grandchildren. I am quite happy here, you know."

EMPIRE WINDRUSH

LONDON

Guest workers

The economies of **developed countries** pull in economic migrants from less-developed countries. The **immigrants** may plan to stay only for a short time, but they often settle down permanently.

Migration within Europe

During the economic boom in western Europe in the 1950s and 1960s, many people were still living and working in the countryside. **Agriculture** has cycles of prosperity and depression like any other industry, but even at the best of times wages are often lower than in the manufacturing industry. So people left behind low wages in **rural** areas for better paid jobs in the cities. Sometimes the **migration** was within one country. In Italy, for example, many people migrated from poor, rural southern Italy to the prosperous **industrial** cities of northern Italy. Sometimes the migrants moved to a different country. They moved from poor, rural Ireland to the cities of Britain, from Spain and Portugal to France, and from Italy to Switzerland.

Gastarbeiter

One of the biggest and most successful economies in the 1950s and 1960s was that of West Germany. People from southern Europe, and especially Turkey, migrated there to work. The Germans called them *gastarbeiter*, which means 'guest workers'. They wanted to make it clear that the workers

The red arrow shows the movement of *gastarbeiter*, or guest workers, from Turkey to West Germany in the 1950s and 1960s.

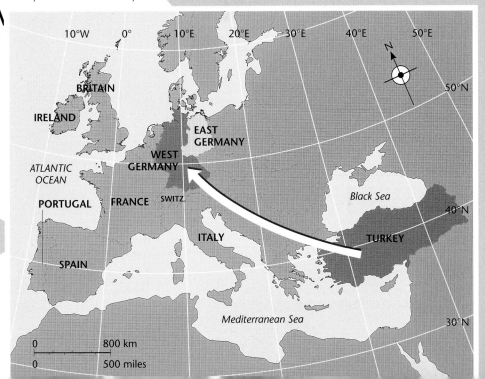

This Hispanic woman is harvesting apples in California, USA.

were temporary visitors, not permanent residents. Many migrants worked this way, not just the Turks in Germany. Only the men would move, and they would return home to their families for holidays, or permanently once they had saved enough money. Between 1955 and 1973, 5,100,000 foreigners worked in Germany.

Settling down

Gradually, guest workers began to settle down more or less permanently in their adopted countries. The back-and-forth way of life was unsettling, and there were jobs for women as well as men, so men brought their wives to stay. Soon there were children born in the new country, going to school there and learning the language. Families who lived in their adopted country all the time, and paid the taxes, gained the rights of citizens. But even when Turks had learned German, they were different from their neighbours in another way, because most of them were Muslims. With **immigration**, and natural growth in the immigrant community, there are now just over 3 million Muslims in Germany, making up 3.7 per cent of the population.

Mexicans in the USA

The USA, with the world's largest economy, has attracted millions of economic migrants from Mexico. They have often entered the country illegally, across the long land border between the two countries. Many are seasonal workers in agriculture. But, like the guest workers in Europe, many have settled down. They are part of a large group of Spanish-speaking US immigrants known as **Hispanics**. Hispanic people have more children than is average in the USA. With immigration and natural growth, the Hispanic population of the USA is 37 million. There are more Hispanics than African Americans.

Consider this:
no going back

The European economy has changed. Spain, Portugal, and Ireland are much more prosperous. Germany now has high levels of unemployment. In 2003 the rate was 8.7 per cent. But the government cannot solve the unemployment problem by simply sending the *gastarbeiter* back to Turkey. The first generation are old enough to retire, on pensions which they have been paying for throughout their working lives; the next generation are German-born citizens

chapter four

The issues

Left behind

What happens in the places the migrants have left? How big is the effect there? That depends on how many people **migrate**, how long they stay away, and whether they are mainly men or women.

How many migrants?

When only a few people leave, the gap is soon filled by population growth. A poor community may see each migrant as one less mouth to feed. But when large numbers leave, it can be a problem for the community. There may be an elderly population with few people left to care for them.

Temporary migrants

The community that is left behind is also affected by temporary migration. Very often only the men migrate, but sometimes it is the women. Mexican migration to the USA, and Turkish migration to Germany, started in this way. Many Irish men work on British building sites during the summer months. This kind of migration is also very common within **developing countries**. Another cause of seasonal migration is the need for a labour force to pick crops. You can find out more about seasonal workers in *People on the Move: Nomads and Travellers*.

There is a long tradition of men from **rural** southern Africa finding work in the big cities of South Africa, in the gold mines, diamond mines, and factories. This is permanent work, not seasonal, and the men go home to their families only for brief holidays, or for a weekend every month. They leave behind a community of older people, mothers, and children. The women struggle to keep the family farm going and to bring up the children

Philippino migrant workers in Hong Kong gather in a city square on their day off.

without a father. This is difficult enough when the jobs are reliable, and men send money home regularly. But if the man loses his job, or makes a new life with a new family in the city, the family back home is left in poverty.

Consider this:
half a family

Can you imagine being a father, or a mother, knowing that the only way you could support your family and educate your children was to see so little of them? This way of life is difficult both for the migrant and for the family left behind. Whenever they can, migrants bring their families to join them.

Women-only migration

Women in developing countries also migrate to find work in the cities of their own country, or in richer countries. They often work as domestic servants and nannies for well-off families. There are 240,000 women from the Philippines in Hong Kong. They work as *amahs* — servants and nannies. They send almost all their wages home to support their families. The Philippine government estimates that about 10 per cent of the country's 75 million people work overseas in order to support their families. Overseas workers are one of the country's biggest exports, with large numbers going to America, Japan, and Saudi Arabia as well as Hong Kong.

This woman from Mashabela, South Africa, describes how her family is divided by temporary migration.

"My name is Mamadile Terdla Mohuba. I am a primary school teacher, teaching children aged 9 and upwards. I have three children -- two girls, aged five and twelve, and a boy aged eight. My husband lives in Pretoria. He works as a technical assistant in the Transvaal museum and only comes home at the end of the month. We have lived like that ever since we were first married."

In a new country

What impact do migrants have on the place they move to? The main effect is on the people who are already living there.

Before the migrants

All the **migrations** we have looked at have been to places which were already inhabited. There may have been as many as 20 million Native Americans living in North America when Christopher Columbus arrived in 1492. When Britain claimed Australia as a **colony** in 1788, there were 700,000 Aboriginal People living there. Yet there was room for millions of settlers in both places. One reason for this was that the **indigenous** people were thinly spread out. Many settlers thought of them as primitive savages. Their rights to the land could be ignored, so the settlers could act as if it was empty.

Emptying the land

Sometimes, shamefully, settlers deliberately attacked and killed indigenous people. Local people also suffered terribly when they caught diseases from settlers to which they had no resistance. When Captain Cook reached Hawaii in 1778, there were about half a million people living there. By 1853 the population had been reduced to 84,000 by diseases such as tuberculosis, influenza, and typhoid. Similar tragedies happened throughout North and South America, and in Australia. Germs and viruses often spread faster through the native population than the European explorers. The effects of disease added to the settlers' impression that the land was empty. Then the survivors were pushed off the land by the law. Under the Allotment Act of 1887, Native Americans lost 86 million acres of land. They were pushed onto **reservations** on the worst land.

And filling it again

Before long, the settlers had filled the empty land. But still the **immigrants** came. The westward drift of the American population created room for new arrivals from Europe. New immigrants bought farms from older immigrants, who headed out west to

Native American buffalo hunters were pushed from the Great Plains by settlers from the east.

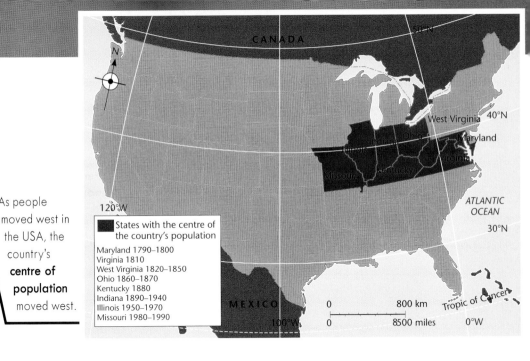

As people moved west in the USA, the country's **centre of population** moved west.

States with the centre of the country's population

Maryland 1790–1800
Virginia 1810
West Virginia 1820–1850
Ohio 1860–1870
Kentucky 1880
Indiana 1890–1940
Illinois 1950–1970
Missouri 1980–1990

CANADA

West Virginia 40°N
Maryland
Ohio
Missouri
Kentucky
Virginia

ATLANTIC OCEAN

30°N

120°W
100°W

MEXICO

Tropic of Cancer

0   800 km
0   8500 miles   0°W

start a new farm. And many immigrants went to the growing cities, where they lived in the cheapest areas. As they became established and prospered, they moved into better areas, leaving room for the next wave of immigrants.

Waves of difference

As the pattern of push factors changed, migrants came from different places. They brought new languages, cultures, and lifestyles. Catholic Irish, Italians, and Poles, and later millions of Jews, added to the American mix of faiths. More recently, millions of Spanish-speaking people, from Mexico and Central America, have migrated to the USA. They can earn in an hour what many Mexicans earn in a whole day. **Hispanics** are now the country's largest minority. East Los Angeles, with a population that is 90 per cent Hispanic, is the second-largest Spanish-speaking community in the world. After many years in which immigrants to Australia came almost entirely from Britain, more recently they have come from southern Europe and Asia.

Consider this:
guilt and survival

Today most people agree that Aboriginal People and Native Americans suffered terrible injustice at the hands of white settlers. People have also become more concerned about the harmful effects we are having on the environment. They point out that indigenous people lived in harmony with the land for thousands of years. While indigenous people are still among the poorest in their countries, their numbers, and pride in their traditional cultures have been increasing.

Economic migrants: benefits and costs

Are the **immigrants** welcome? One way to answer this is to look at the economic benefits and costs that migrants bring to their adopted home.

Economic benefits

Most **developed countries** now have a low **birth rate**. At the same time, people are living longer. Therefore the average age of the population is rising, and a larger proportion of the population is elderly and retired. **Economies** need people of working age to keep them running. Economic migrants are usually young adults, with a full working life ahead of them, so they make a valuable contribution. Immigrants are often prepared to do the jobs that comfortably-off residents will not do. These include manual work, work with unsocial hours, and low-paid work.

Immigrants may bring useful skills and be able to fill skills shortages. They may also, in their enthusiasm to make a success of their new life, have ideas for new businesses which stimulate the economy and create jobs. They have taken the risk of **migrating,** so they are ready to take risks in setting up a new business. The film industry started in Hollywood because a Jewish immigrant, Sam Goldwyn, went there to build a studio. Jewish immigrants also founded some famous High Street names in Britain, such as Tesco, Marks and Spencer, and Burtons. One of the causes of the USA's fast economic growth in the 1990s was the 13.5 million people who **immigrated** in that decade.

Immigrants often take low-paid jobs with unsocial hours, that no-one else will do.

Economic costs

The disadvantages of economic migrants for the new country are more complicated. During the Great Migration to the USA in the 19th century, working people resented immigrants because they feared they would compete for jobs and push wages down. For the same reason, employers encouraged immigration, and even printed leaflets about the attractions of the USA, to distribute in Europe. In fact the economy was usually growing so fast that there were enough new jobs for the millions of immigrants. But it is true that immigrants may take jobs that would otherwise go to local people.

Consider this:
what is the real issue?

Sometimes immigrants make convenient scapegoats to blame for complicated economic problems that go beyond immigration. And sometimes people who are opposed to immigration describe it as an economic problem, although it has benefits as well as costs. For many people, the real problems about immigration are to do with language, culture, and race, as we will see over the page.

Nowadays, when most rich countries have **social security** systems, there is a concern that immigrants will come and claim **benefits**. It is true that this is possible. However, if people have migrated for economic reasons, they will want to make as much money as possible. They will prefer to work because they can earn more than they receive in benefits.

Another cost arises if there are many immigrants with young families who do not speak the language of the host country. Schools have to teach the immigrants' children a new language before they can begin to teach them anything else. This may mean employing extra teachers to avoid disrupting the education of local children.

Notices in the languages of immigrants are common sights in the schools of many British cities.

اپنا ایپرن یہاں لٹکائیں

Hang up your apron here.

Integration and diversity

Economic migration often brings in people whose language, religion, or race are different from those of the host country. How quickly, and how completely, will they **integrate** with the majority?

Integration in the USA

The great European **migration** to the USA in the 19th century brought in people who spoke many languages. **Immigrants** from the same country naturally stayed together at first, but soon they began to mix. They may have kept their religion, and their food, but they lived and worked in integrated communities.

Restricting immigration into the USA

The idea of integration was challenged when immigrants arrived from China and Japan. They were visibly of a different race. **Discrimination** based on race was very common in the 19th century. The USA banned Chinese **immigration** for ten years in 1882. Further laws passed between 1917 and 1924 reduced all immigration to about 150,000 a year. Eighty per cent of permitted admissions were to be from northern and western Europe.

British immigration controls

Immigration became a political issue later in Britain. The race and culture of the Black and Asian immigrants of the 1950s and 1960s were conspicuously different from those of the white majority. Britain placed restrictions on immigration from former **colonies** in 1962.

The annual Notting Hill Carnival has brought the Caribbean carnival tradition to London, so that both black and white people can celebrate together.

The dilemma

It would be easy to dismiss these reactions as merely racist. Very few people today would defend racism. But it is not racist to ask how large-scale immigration affects national identity. If you are born in Germany of Turkish parents, speak fluent German and perhaps little or no Turkish, are you a German or a Turk? It is the dilemma of the immigrant everywhere, and through the ages, and also for the host nation. It is especially difficult when a host nation is at war with a country from which it has received many immigrants. The loyalty of German-Americans was questioned when the USA was at war with Germany in 1917–1918 and Japanese Americans were **interned** when the USA was at war with Japan in 1941–1945 because they were thought not to be trustworthy.

This Muslim family live in Hanover, Germany.

Cultural diversity

What if some immigrants do not want to integrate? The integration of different cultural groups is becoming a political issue. For example, France passed a controversial law in 2004 banning girls from wearing the Muslim *hijab*, a headscarf, in schools, on the grounds that schools are non-religious places. The law also banned pupils from wearing a cross, the symbol of Christianity. But opponents of the law saw it as an attack on personal choice and religious freedom.

In the USA, it took many years for the idea of integration to be extended to African Americans. Now a different challenge to integration comes from the **Hispanic** population. The USA is a nation of immigrants, but has never had such a big group of migrants with their own language and culture. Where they form a large minority, gathered together in neighbourhoods, there is less need for them to learn English. There are Spanish media, and politicians speak Spanish to appeal to Hispanic voters. Some people fear that the Hispanic community will remain separate, especially as immigration from Spanish-speaking countries in Central America remains high.

chapter five

Conclusion

Diverse societies

In this book we have seen some big **migrations**, which changed life for ever for the people who made the journey. These migrations made the world in which we live now. **Immigration** makes countries interesting and diverse. People celebrate Hanukah, Christmas, Eid, Chinese New Year, and Diwali. In this, and in many other ways, we live in diverse societies, especially in the big cities. We have all been affected by **economic migration**, even if our family has lived in the same place for ever.

Your decision

Some of the push and pull factors which we have seen in this book may affect you. You may have to decide whether your situation is likely to get better or worse, and whether a move will be worth making. You may move across the country, or across the world, to find a better job. If you move far, you may find yourself among unfamiliar people, having to learn new ways, perhaps a new language. You would hope to be made welcome.

New neighbours

You may find **immigrants** living near you. The push and pull factors that make people migrate are probably stronger now than at any time in history. The gap between rich and poor countries is bigger than ever, and still growing. The push factors of war and oppression show no sign of decreasing. The new immigrants in your street may have come from the other side of your country, or from the other side of the world. Will you make them feel welcome? You will have to decide how to react personally, and what to think about immigration, which has become a controversial political issue.

Migrants and the grandchildren of migrants mix on the streets of big cities in **developed countries**.

Illegal immigrants

In February 2004, at least nineteen illegal Chinese immigrant workers drowned while picking cockles in Morecambe Bay, England. The tragedy brought to light that there may be as many as 70,000 Chinese working illegally in Britain. The government gives up to 200,000 work permits to economic migrants every year, but there are probably hundreds of thousands more illegal migrants working in Britain.

The US government estimated that there were 7 million illegal immigrants in the country in 2000. One and a half million had entered before 1990, and 5.5 million entered in the 1990s. Mexicans make up 69 per cent of this total, with 4.8 million people. California had 2.2 million illegal immigrants, or 32 per cent of the total. Other states with many illegal immigrants were Texas, New York, Illinois, and Florida.

Governments faced with illegal immigration on this scale have to answer three questions:

• is immigration good for the country?
• what is the right level of legal immigration?
• how can we prevent illegal immigration?

Consider this:
me, a migrant?

At some point in your family history someone was probably an economic migrant. Try to find out how far back you have to go in your family to find them. Where did they come from, and why? If you draw a blank, ask around among your friends. You might find some fascinating stories.

Statistics:

Immigrant countries

These figures show the population in countries which have received many **immigrants**. The increases include natural population growth as well as **immigration**.

Australia

Year	Immigrant population
1788	0
1840	130,000
1860	1,000,000
2002	19,500,000

New Zealand

Year	Immigrant population
1837	0
2002	3,317,000

USA

Year	Population
1790	3,893,874
1800	5,236,631
1810	7,036,509
1820	10,037,323
1830	12,785,928
1840	16,987,946
1850	23,054,152
1860	31,183,582
1870	38,155,505
1880	49,371,340
1890	62,116,811
1900	75,994,575
1910	91,972,266
1920	105,710,620
1930	122,775,046
1940	131,669,275
1950	150,697,361
1960	179,323,175
1970	203,211,926
1980	226,545,805
1990	248,709,873
2000	281,421,906

Argentina

Between 1857 and 1930 Argentina welcomed 3.5 million immigrants. In 1914, when 13 per cent of the population of the USA was foreign-born, the proportion in Argentina was 30 per cent. Italians made up 46 per cent of the migrants, and Spaniards 32 per cent.

Immigrant communities from former colonies

France had **colonies** in the Caribbean and in Africa, especially Algeria. The Netherlands' colonies were Indonesia and Surinam. Both countries had large numbers of immigrants from ex-colonies. In France, where many migrants were from Muslim North Africa, the Muslims now make up 10 per cent of the population,

and there are 870,000 Muslims in Holland, making 5.4 per cent of the population.

Germany

Unemployment figures provide a measure of how well the **economy** is doing. When unemployment is low, economic migrants will be attracted to the country. In the early 1970s, unemployment rose and fewer economic migrants moved there.

Year	% unemployment
1955	3.9
1960	0.9
1965	0.5
1970	0.4
1971	0.5
1972	0.7
1973	0.8
1974	1.3
1975	2.3

The table below shows how many foreigners were living in Germany in 2002. In total there were 7,296,817 foreigners living in Germany, making up almost 9 per cent of the total population of 82 million.

Country of origin	Number, December 2002
Turkey	1,998,534
Yugoslavia (Serbia/ Montenegro)	662,495
Bosnia Herzegovina	156,294
Poland	301,366
Croatia	216,827
Russia	115,856
Iran	107,927
Romania	90,094
Ukraine	89,282
Vietnam	89,138
Morocco	80,226
Afghanistan	72,199
Iraq	60,913
Sri Lanka	50,579
Hungary	54,437
Lebanon	51,375
China	50,885
Tunisia	24,316

Temporary migrants

In 2003, Mexicans working in the USA sent home $13 billion, and workers from El Salvador sent $2 billion. In total, **Hispanic** workers living in industrialized countries sent home $38 billion. The global total may be as high as $80 billion a year.

People trafficking

Women trafficked across borders every year: 900,000. Money made from this every year: $12 billion (£6.6 billion).

Emigrant countries

The following tables show the number of people leaving each country as **emigrants,** most of them to the USA.

Britain

Year	Number of emigrants
1820–1830	30,000 per year
1830–1840	60,000 per year
1832	100,000
1842	130,000
1849	300,000
1851-71	3,700,000 in total

Italy

Year	Number of emigrants
1869	119,806
1875	103,348
1880	119,901
1885	157,193
1891	293,631
1896	307,482
1900	352,782

Internal migrations in the USA

These figures show the increase in the population of the western states as people moved westward during the 20th century.

Western state	Population in 1900	Population in 2000
Arizona	122,931	5,130,632
California	1,485,053	33,871,648
Nevada	42,335	1,998,257
Oregon	413,536	3,421,399
Washington	518,103	5,894,121

These figures illustrate how **migration** has created a multi-racial society in the USA. They show the percentages of the population that were of different racial groups, both in California and in the whole USA.

Racial group	% in California in 2000	% in USA in 2000
Black or African American Indians and Alaska Natives	6.7	12.3
	1.0	0.9
Asians	10.9	3.6
Other race	16.8	5.5
Two or more races	4.7	2.4
Hispanic or Latino	32.4	12.5

Illegal immigration

These are the ten states of the USA with the highest number of illegal immigrants, in 2000.

State	Number of illegal immigrants in 2000
California	2,209,000
Texas	1,041,000
New York	489,000
Illinois	432,000
Florida	337,000
Arizona	283,000
Georgia	228,000
New Jersey	221,000
North Carolina	206,000
Colorado	144,000

These are the ten countries where most of the illegal immigrants to the USA came from.

Country	Number of illegal immigrants in 2000
Mexico	4,808,000
El Salvador	189,000
Guatemala	144,000
Colombia	141,000
Honduras	138,000
China	115,000
Ecuador	108,000
Dominican Republic	91,000
Philippines	85,000
Brazil	77,000

Urbanization in developing countries

These figures show the increase between 1980 and 2002 in the percentage of each country's population that was living in cities. Between 1990 and 1995 cities in **developing countries** grew by 263 million people.

Country	% of population urbanized in 1980	% of population urbanized in 2002
Bangladesh	15	26
Cameroon	31	50
Gabon	50	83
Mexico	66	75
Philippines	37	60
Tanzania	15	34
Zimbabwe	22	37

These were the five most highly populated cities in the world in 2000.

City	Population
Tokyo, Japan	26,400,000
Mexico City, Mexico	18,100,000
Bombay, India	18,100,000
São Paulo, Brazil	17,800,000
New York, USA	16,600,000

Map of migration routes

The arrows on this map of the world show some of the major migration routes discussed in the book.

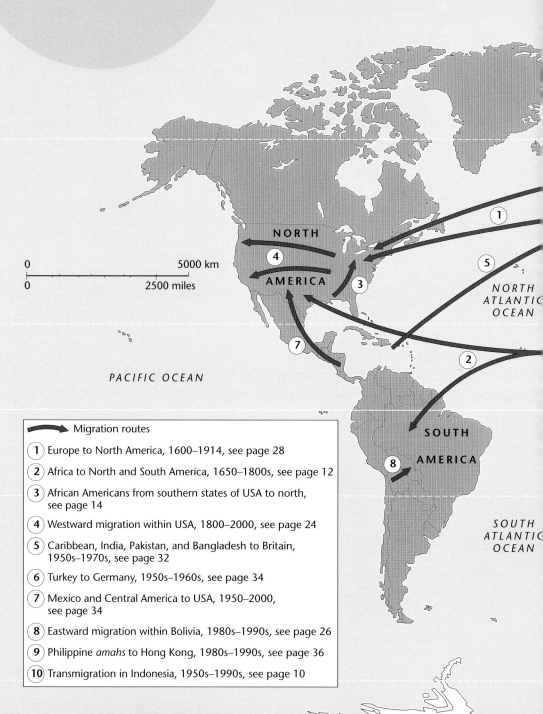

NORTH AMERICA

0 ——————————————— 5000 km
0 ——————————————— 2500 miles

PACIFIC OCEAN

NORTH ATLANTIC OCEAN

SOUTH AMERICA

SOUTH ATLANTIC OCEAN

➤ Migration routes

1 Europe to North America, 1600–1914, see page 28

2 Africa to North and South America, 1650–1800s, see page 12

3 African Americans from southern states of USA to north, see page 14

4 Westward migration within USA, 1800–2000, see page 24

5 Caribbean, India, Pakistan, and Bangladesh to Britain, 1950s–1970s, see page 32

6 Turkey to Germany, 1950s–1960s, see page 34

7 Mexico and Central America to USA, 1950–2000, see page 34

8 Eastward migration within Bolivia, 1980s–1990s, see page 26

9 Philippine *amahs* to Hong Kong, 1980s–1990s, see page 36

10 Transmigration in Indonesia, 1950s–1990s, see page 10

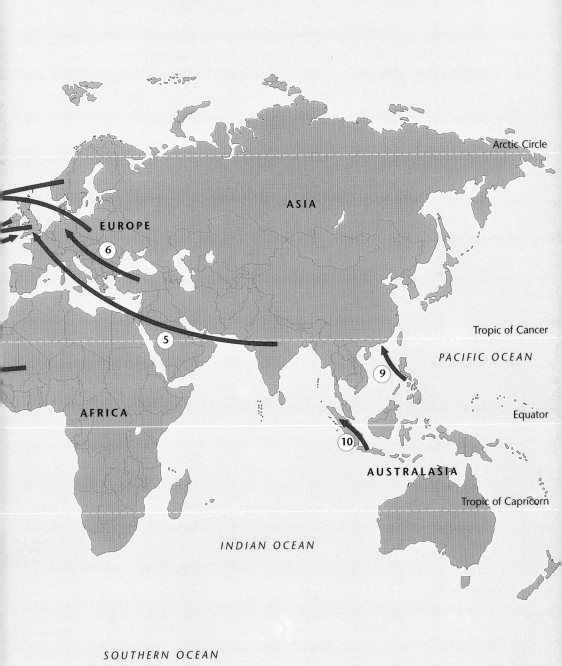

Arctic Circle

ASIA

EUROPE

6

5

Tropic of Cancer

PACIFIC OCEAN

9

AFRICA

Equator

10

AUSTRALASIA

Tropic of Capricorn

INDIAN OCEAN

SOUTHERN OCEAN

Antarctic Circle

ANTARCTICA

Timeline of key events and migrations

1492	Columbus journeys to the **New World**
1607	the first British settlement is established in North America, at Jamestown, Virginia
1619	the first black slaves are sold in Virginia
1648–1815	9 million slaves are taken from Africa to the New World
1788	a British **colony** is established in Australia
1803	USA buys Louisiana from France and doubles in size
1807	Britain outlaws the slave trade, and USA outlaws slave imports
1819	USA buys Florida from Spain
1837	a British colony is established in New Zealand
1840–1850	**economic depression** in Britain and Ireland, **emigration** increases
1845–1848	USA gains territory between Texas and California from Mexico
1848	gold is discovered in California
1851	gold is discovered in Australia
1862	Homestead Act, USA: each pioneer family can have 160 acres free, if they farm the land for five years
1869	Union Pacific railway, going west and built by Irish **immigrants**, meets Central Pacific railway going east and built by Chinese immigrants, at Promontory Point, Utah
1882	Chinese Exclusion Act stops Chinese **immigration** to the USA for ten years
	European immigration to the USA peaks at 788,992
1888–1898	Brazil receives 1.25 million immigrants, mainly Italians
1905–1914	European immigration to the USA reaches an average 1 million a year
1914–1918	World War I closes off European **migration** to the USA. African Americans from the southern states migrate to find factory jobs in the north.

1917–1924	USA passes laws to restrict immigration
1924–1933	110,000 Japanese migrate to Brazil
1929	Wall Street Crash – start of the Great Depression in the USA
1932	unemployment reaches 25 per cent in the USA, 22.9 per cent in Britain
1930–1940	migration to California, where the state population grows by 1,230,000
	migration to London, south-east, and Midlands from areas of high unemployment in the rest of Britain
1941	140,000 Japanese Americans in the USA are **interned** during the World War II
1948	first immigrants arrive in Britain from the colonies
1955–1970	German **economy** booms and Turkish workers migrate to Germany
1962	Commonwealth Immigration Act restricts immigration to Britain, the first of a series of Acts which increasingly restrict immigration from the ex-colonies
1964	California becomes the most highly populated state of the USA
1969–1989	during **transmigration** in Indonesia 730,000 families move from Java to other islands
1972	Australia changes the 'White Australia' policy, and allows immigration from Asia
1988	Australia has 16 million people, 25 per cent of them immigrants
1990–1995	cities of the **developing** world grow by 263 million people
1990–2000	immigration to USA reaches 13.5 million, 3.5 million of them are illegal
2004	ten new states enter the European Union. Britain imposes restrictions on **economic migrants** from these states.

Glossary

agriculture farming. An agricultural economy is one in which most people live in the countryside and make their living from farming.

benefits payments from the government to individuals, in a social security system. For instance, people who have lost their jobs may get unemployment benefit.

birth rate number of children born in a country. The rate is usually measured in births per thousand adults.

centre of population If you look at a flat map of a country, imagine putting identical weights on it, so that each weight represents a person at the place they are living at a certain time. The centre of population would be the point on which the map would balance.

civil rights a person's rights as a citizen, for example to vote in elections, to fair trial, to hold an opinion, speak your mind, and join organizations

colony country ruled by the government of another, more powerful, country

developed country a relatively rich country that has experienced economic development

developing country a country that is not yet rich. It may be very poor.

discrimination treating someone less favourably because of their sex, race, or religion

economic depression time when a country's economy is not doing well. Businesses fail, unemployment is high, confidence and investment are low.

economic migration migration for economic reasons, such as to find work

economy a country's economy is created by the work people do, the money they spend, and the goods and services they produce

emigrant someone who migrates out of a country

emigration migration out of a country

gastarbeiter German word meaning 'guest worker', a temporary economic immigrant

Hispanic a person of Spanish-speaking descent

immigrant someone who migrates into a country

immigration migration into a country

indigenous indigenous people are the original people of a country, before migration. For instance the Aboriginal People were the indigenous people of Australia.

industrial an industrial economy is one in which most things are made in factories, and most people work in industry, not in agriculture. Industrialization is the change in a country's economy from mainly agricultural to mainly industrial.

integration   immigrants adopting the language and ways of their new country

internal migration   migration from one part of a country to another, or from the countryside to a city

interned   put in a prison or secure camp by the government, even though you have not been convicted of a crime

migration   movement of people, especially in large numbers, from one country to another, or from one part of a country to another

New World   North, South, and Central America, in contrast to Europe, Asia and Africa

persecution   to be abused or robbed of your rights because of your religion or race

pig iron   raw iron ore is blasted in a furnace to make pig iron, or blocks, which can then be used for making steel

plantation   big farm, usually in a colony, growing one crop for sale, and often worked by slaves

reservation   area set aside for a group of people to live in, especially for Native Americans in the USA

rural   to do with the countryside and the agricultural way of life

sanitation   safe, clean ways of dealing with human waste

scapegoat   person who is blamed for something even though it is not their fault

segregation   keeping people of different races apart, for instance by providing separate schools

shares   people can buy shares in a company. These entitle the owner to receive a share of the profits that the company makes. If the company is doing well, the price of its shares will go up. If it is doing badly, the price will fall.

social security   money paid by governments in developed countries to citizens, depending on their circumstances. For example, pensions are paid to old people and people with disabilities, and unemployment benefit to people without work.

Stock Market   place where people trade company shares. The New York Stock Market is sometimes known as Wall Street.

transmigration   policy of the Indonesian government encouraging people to migrate from the crowded islands, such as Java, to other islands such as Sumatra

urban   to do with towns and cities. Urbanization is the growth of cities and the movement of people to cities, and an urbanized country has a high proportion of its population living in town and cities.

Further resources

Places to visit

The Wilberforce House Museum, High Street, Hull
Wilberforce led the movement in the UK to abolish the slave trade, and this museum, based in his home, contains documents and artefacts relating to the slave trade and its abolition. It also has a website:
www.hullcc.gov.uk/wilberforce/index.html

Websites

International Organization for Migration
www.iom.int

Centre for Migration Studies, New York
www.cmsny.org

National Centre for Migration Studies, University of Aberdeen, Scotland
www.ini.smo.uhi.ac.uk/contact.htm

Web pages about the Windrush immigrants of 1948
www.bbc.co.uk/history/society_culture/multicultural/arrival_01.shtml

A German site (but with English-language pages) on Turkish migrants to Germany
www.domit.de/

The British Refugee Council supports refugees and campaigns for decent treatment of refugees
www.refugeecouncil.org.uk/index.htm

Anti-Slavery International campaigns against slavery in the modern world
www.antislavery.org

Worldaware works in the UK to raise awareness of international development issues
www.worldaware.org.uk

Worldaware's sites for schools
www.globaleye.org.uk

Department of Immigration and Multicultural and Indigenous Affairs in Australia
www.immi.gov.au

Immigration Museum in Melbourne, Australia
www.immigration.museum.vic.gov.au

Research your own family history
Why not type your family name into a search engine and see if you can find migrants in your family's history?

Further reading
Bowden, Rob, *Just the Facts: World Poverty*, (Heinemann Library, 2002)

Dalton, Dave, *People on the Move: Environmental Migrants*, (Heinemann Library, 2006)

Dalton, Dave, *People on the Move: Nomads and Travellers*, (Heinemann Library, 2006)

Dalton, Dave, *People on the Move: Refugees and Asylum Seekers*, (Heinemann Library, 2006)

Harris, Nathaniel, *Witness to History: The Great Depression*, (Heinemann Library, 2003)

Horton, Edward, *Nations of the World: Indonesia*, (Raintree, 2004)

Emma Lazarus wrote this poem about the Statue of Liberty in 1883. In 1903, a group of people paid to have it cast in bronze and attached to the statue.

The New Colossus
Not like the brazen giant of Greek fame,
With conquering limbs astride from land to land:
Here at our sea-washed, sunset gates shall stand
A mighty woman with a torch, whose flame
Is the imprisoned lightning, and her name
Mother of Exiles. From her beacon-hand
Glows world-wide welcome; her mild eyes command
The air-bridged harbor that twin cities frame.
"Keep, ancient lands, your storied pomp!" cries she
With silent lips. "Give me your tired, your poor,
Your huddled masses yearning to breathe free,
The wretched refuse of your teeming shore.
Send these, the homeless, tempest-tost to me.
I lift my lamp beside the golden door."
Emma Lazarus, 1883

Index